SEVEN REASONS WHY BAD THINGS HAPPEN TO GOOD PEOPLE

Dave Bisbee

A summary of this book and the order page can be accessed here: *www.genesisapologetics.com/why-do-bad-things-happen-to-good-people/*

Seven Reasons Why Bad Things Happen to Good People
by Dave Bisbee

Printed in the United States of America

ISBN-9798351581675

Print Version September 2022

Dedication

To my wife Connie, who has stood faithfully by my side for over 35 years. Thank you for your steadfast love and support—especially during the hard times. Thanks for having the courage to tell me what I need to hear and encouraging me to listen to God.

I would also like to thank Dan Biddle and Mark Johnson for their encouragement, friendship and loyalty over the last twenty years. Thank you for mentoring me and helping me grow stronger in my faith.

Finally, I would like to thank the Lord for not giving up on me. Thank you for saving me and giving me the honor and privilege of serving You.

Contents

About the Author

David A. Bisbee is the Vice President of Genesis Apologetics, Inc., a non-profit 501c3 organization that equips Christian students attending public schools and their parents with faith-building materials that reaffirm a Biblical creation worldview. Genesis Apologetics is committed to providing Christian families with Biblically-and scientifically-based answers to the evolutionary theory that students are taught in public schools.

Mr. Bisbee's professional experience includes over 32 years in the field of energy efficiency. For 20 years, he managed a research program which tested energy efficiency technologies in real-world environments. Mr. Bisbee has presented the results of these projects through numerous published reports and educational seminars throughout the United States. Dave recently retired from his secular job to serve in ministry full-time.

Dave's ministry experience includes 20 years of teaching Sunday school classes and creation science presentations. Over the years, he has taught thousands of students. Dave earned his Bachelor of Science degree in Organizational Leadership and a minor in Biblical Studies from William Jessup University.

About the Ministry

Genesis Apologetics is a non-profit 501(c)(3) ministry that equips Christian students and their parents with faith-building materials that affirm a Biblical Creation worldview. We are committed to providing Christian families with Biblically and scientifically accurate answers to the evolutionary theory that public schools propagate. Our doctrinal position on Biblical Creation aligns with Answers in Genesis and the Institute for Creation Research (ICR), which take

Genesis at face value, including its testimony of a miraculous creation and Flood that occurred thousands, not millions of years ago. Genesis Apologetics offers the following free online training resources:

- *Mobile App:* Search for "Genesis Apologetics" in the iTunes or Google Play stores.
- *www.debunkevolution.com*
- *www.genesisapologetics.com*
- YouTube Channel (**Genesis Apologetics**). Our channel includes over 100 videos that promote Biblical Creation.

Foreword

By Daniel Arthur Biddle, Ph.D.

Living in this side of history—after the Fall—is hard. But we have *hope*. Hope in Christ. Hope in Scripture. Hope in an eternal home, Heaven. So, we should "leave it all on the field" in this life. Play it all out, using our time, talent, and treasure for His Kingdom. God is good. You can *trust* Him.

In this work, Dave outlines seven reasons why "bad things happen to good people." Let me comment on each of these from a strategic standpoint—that is, how we can best respond to each.

Fallen World. Realize that things will get messy in this life, but He is still ultimately in control and knows what will happen to you: "Are not two sparrows sold for a copper coin? And not one of them falls to the ground apart from your Father's will" (Mark 10:29). Because this world is broken, life will get complex sometimes. Embrace the complexity, knowing that God is watching.

Free Will. Yes, we have free will. But God is still in control. Don't even try to understand how complex these two truths are! Jeremiah 17:10 states, "I, the Lord, search the heart, I test the mind, even to give every man according to his ways, according to the fruit of his doings." God is watching. Live life to please him. When we sin, we ultimately have a *faith* problem, more so than a temptation problem. Would you sin if you really knew Jesus as a real being was right there next to you watching? Therefore, live for an audience of One.

Spiritual Warfare. I have come to realize there are two categories of Christians: those who know and believe that the spirit world is real and live like it, and those who don't. If we could peel back the dimensions and see into the unseen realm, we would be shocked at the reality of what would be uncovered. I *know* this based on my experience and training as a behavioral scientist and I know it from Scripture. We need to live under the

11

direction of Ephesians 6:12–13: "For we do not wrestle against flesh and blood, but against principalities, against powers, against the rulers of the darkness of this age, against spiritual hosts of wickedness in the heavenly places. Therefore take up the whole armor of God, that you may be able to withstand in the evil day, and having done all, to stand."

Bad Choices/Decisions. We all make bad decisions. The older I get the more I realize I don't want to tangle up my time, talent, and treasure with worldly pursuits that end in temporary outcomes. I also don't want to waste my time by repeating mistakes. "There's only one life, this soon will pass, only what's done for Christ will last." Therefore, live by Hebrews 12:1–2: "We also, since we are surrounded by so great a cloud of witnesses, let us lay aside every weight, and the sin which so easily ensnares us, and let us run with endurance the race that is set before us, looking unto Jesus, the author and finisher of our faith, who for the joy that was set before Him endured the cross, despising the shame, and has sat down at the right hand of the throne of God." Also, please remember: there is a different between guilt and shame. Don't shame yourself for making bad choices! As long as you're wrapped in a physical body, you will make bad choices! Forgive yourself.

Test and Grow Our Faith. Philippians 1:6 states, "being confident of this very thing, that He who has begun a good work in you will complete it until the day of Jesus Christ." God is sovereign. He gets to choose *how* to build our faith. In His wisdom, He allows pain and suffering to be part (but not all) of this process. Remember these two key verses: "We also glory in tribulations, knowing that tribulation produces perseverance; and perseverance, character; and character, hope. Now hope does not disappoint, because the love of God has been poured out in our hearts by the Holy Spirit who was given to us" (Romans 5:3–5). James 1:2–4: "My brethren, count it all joy when you fall into various trials, knowing that the testing of your faith produces patience. But let patience have its perfect work, that you may be perfect and complete, lacking nothing."

Discipline/Punishment. When it comes to pain and suffering, one of the most challenging Scripture passages is Hebrews 12:6–11:

> My son, do not despise the chastening of the Lord, nor be discouraged when you are rebuked by Him; for whom the Lord loves He chastens, and scourges every son whom He receives." If you endure chastening, God deals with you as with sons; for what son is there whom a father does not chasten? But if you are without chastening, of which all have become partakers, then you are illegitimate and not sons. Furthermore, we have had human fathers who corrected us, and we paid them respect. Shall we not much more readily be in subjection to the Father of spirits and live? For they indeed for a few days chastened us as seemed best to them, but He for our profit, that we may be partakers of His holiness. Now no chastening seems to be joyful for the present, but painful; nevertheless, afterward it yields the peaceable fruit of righteousness to those who have been trained by it.

Last year about this time, four things happened within a few weeks' time: I contracted a bad case of COVID, my brother died from liver failure, my mom's cancer return caused her eyes to bulge with tumors, and I became an empty nester with all four kids out of the house. My world was "rocked" more than ever. For weeks my energy was depleted, family support network gone, and my fight left my spirit. Where was God in all of this? Did He cause these things to punish me? No—but He *allowed* them, and I endured them *as* chastisement, regardless of *why* they were happening. I humbled myself. I grew. I re-anchored my Spirit in the Lord. He used these things in my life to re-assemble my root system. During this downtime, He birthed our new movie on Noah's Flood (_www.noahsflood.com_). He did this when I was low and humbled so that His strength and purpose could be much higher than my own. As Paul said in 2 Corinthians 12:9–10: "And He said to me, 'My grace is sufficient for you, for My strength is made perfect in weakness.' Therefore most gladly I will rather boast in my infirmities, that the power of Christ may rest upon me. Therefore I take pleasure in infirmities, in reproaches, in needs, in persecutions, in distresses, for Christ's sake. For when I am weak, then I am strong."

God's Purpose. A friend of mine once said to me, "I can't believe that God is good because of what He did to Job in the Bible." God allowed Job to be tested beyond anyone in history. Satan took away everything from Job—his health, family, wealth, business, and everything else. Where is a good starting place to comprehend this? Perhaps it's to first realize that _it's all His to begin with._ Giving these back to Him is a wise response. Starting here brings gratefulness to our souls.

Chapter 1: Introduction

"But in your hearts revere Christ as Lord. Always be prepared to give an answer to everyone who asks you to give the reason for the hope that you have. But do this with gentleness and respect" (1 Peter 3:15).

The lesson had gone well. Over 50 middle school students had attended the session and they were very engaged. Best of all, four students had responded to the gospel invitation! The next session would start in 10 minutes and I was busy arranging the dinosaur fossils. Then I noticed him. The young man sat quietly in his chair staring at the ground. All of the other students had already left but a teacher's aide was sitting in the back of the room waiting for him.

When I approached the young man and asked him if everything was okay, he looked up and quietly said "not really." When I asked him what was bothering him, he seemed rather embarrassed: "I'm having doubts about my faith, is that okay?"

I told him that having doubts may actually be a good thing. It's important for people to know what they believe and why they believe it. His doubts were an indication that he was starting to develop his own faith instead of riding on the coattails of his parents. Handled properly, he could emerge with a stronger faith. Encouraged, I asked specifically about his doubts and he responded with an age-old question: "If God is good and God is powerful, then why do bad things happen to good people?" Ouch! There are no easy answers to this question and there simply wasn't enough time to adequately discuss it with him. It was this encounter which finally motivated me to sit down and write this book.

The purpose of this book is not to provide ammunition to win arguments against atheists. Nor is it to provide quick, easy answers to very complex situations. This book is primarily intended to share insights and provide some comfort to Christians who are suffering and struggling with their faith. Although some people say "God moves in mysterious ways," this is a totally inadequate response for those who are struggling and seeking answers. We are about to embark upon a journey to seek some answers. Before we start, please note the following cautions:

- We often do not and cannot know the reason(s) why specific events occur. Please do not assume it is always because someone is being punished by God.

- When someone is hurting, please do not try to comfort them with theology! Just be there and love them until they are ready to talk. Of course, the best time to talk about theology is before a crisis hits.

- Many smart theologians have developed explanations regarding why a perfectly good, almighty, and all-knowing God permits evil (theodicy). Although no single idea is sufficient to explain the evil we see happening all around us, God has given us enough information in His Word to create a "mosaic" that provides at least some level of explanation.

Now that we have covered the basics, let's dive in!

Worldview

Theologian and pastor A.W. Tozer once said: "The most important thing about you is what you believe about God."[1] What is your starting point? Do you believe people are wonderful and deserve only good things or do you believe we are totally evil and deserve death? Is God some sort of cosmic genie whose purpose is to make us happy by granting our every wish? Is God angry all the time and constantly looking for someone to punish? Does God want to send people to Hell? Do

16

you truly believe that God is good? How you answer these questions is vitally important because it determines your starting point and has a profound effect on your perspective about life's events.

The Bible tells a story. God created everything and it was very good (Genesis 1:31). God created us in His image (Genesis 1:27) and wants to have a relationship with us (Genesis 3:8). Unfortunately, mankind rebelled against God (Genesis 3) and corrupted God's beautiful creation through our sin (Romans 8:20–21). The paradise that God originally created has been replaced by a battlefield. We now live in a world that includes pain, suffering, and death (Romans 5:12).

Since God is holy and righteous (Revelation 15:3–5) He must punish evil (Isaiah 5:15–17). Because of our sin, we had no hope—we were headed for eternal separation from God. However, since God loves us, He sent his Son to take our punishment (John 3:16). Thanks to Jesus's sacrifice and resurrection from the dead, we now have the opportunity to spend eternity in Heaven by placing our trust in Him. God wants everyone to spend eternity with Him in Heaven (2 Peter 3:9) but leaves this decision up to us (Romans 3:22).

One day Jesus will return and take all believers to be with Him forevermore (1 Thessalonians 4:17). Ultimately, God will judge the wicked. Satan and his demons will be cast into the Lake of Fire (Revelation 20:10). Sadly, so will those who reject God's offer of salvation (Revelation 20:15). After that God will create a new Heaven and Earth and believers from all ages will live together with Him for eternity (Revelation 21:1–7).

That is the basic story of the Bible. The question is: *do you truly believe it?* I hope and pray that you do! The Bible reveals that people and Satan—not God, are to blame for the evil that we see in this world. Knowing that we will one day be in Heaven gives us hope for the future. It changes our perspective and can provide the courage and strength we need to stay faithful to God throughout this journey we call life.

Chapter 2: Fallen World

"For the creation was subjected to frustration, not by its own choice, but by the will of the one who subjected it, in hope that the creation itself will be liberated from its bondage to decay and brought into the freedom and glory of the children of God" (Romans 8:20).

It was Sunday night. Susie and her father were relaxing in the living room. She was watching a show about wildlife in Africa as he read the latest edition of his favorite fishing magazine. As she watched, a hungry lioness attacked a baby zebra that had strayed from the herd. The baby zebra screamed in pain and terror as the sharp teeth and claws of the lioness tore into its flesh. Susie was upset and very confused. Earlier that day her Sunday school teacher taught her that God created the animals and said that everything was good.

"Dad? Is God mean?" she asked. Her father paused for a moment and then asked "What makes you ask Sweetie?" Susie struggled to hold back her tears: "My Sunday school teacher taught us that God made everything and said that it was very good, but that lion was so mean to that baby zebra!" "Lions have got to eat. God made them that way." "Oh, ok," muttered Susie. She turned off the TV and went to her room. As she laid on her bed crying, the first seeds of doubt began to grow.

Sadly, scenes like this happen all too often. Children are taught that God created everything and said it was good. However, when they look at the world around them, they see widespread pain, suffering, and death. Understandably they begin to question what they have been taught. Did God lie? Is He really good? Is God mean? If these questions are not adequately answered, doubts begin to grow and may ultimately destroy the foundation of the child's faith—their belief in the Bible. Children are smart and need the complete story. They need to know that the world today is very different than when God first created it. Let's start by taking a closer look at the first three chapters of Genesis.

Life Before the Fall (Genesis 1 & 2)

When God finished creating everything on day six of Creation Week, He said that everything was *very good* (Genesis 1:31). Here are some of the characteristics of life before the Fall:

- Mankind was given dominion over the earth (Genesis 1:26, 28).
- Work was fulfilling (Genesis 2:15).
- Adam and Eve were very close (Genesis 2:25).
- God walked in the Garden of Eden with Adam and Eve (Genesis 3:8).
- Warm tropical conditions and lush vegetation (confirmed by the presence of extensive fossil fuels).
- Oxygen rich environment (confirmed by huge sauropods in the fossil record with relatively small nostrils and flying reptiles with enormous wingspans. These animals could not exist under today's atmospheric conditions).
- Humans and animals lived a long time.
- Humans and animals were vegetarians.

Consider this passage: "And to all the beasts of the earth and all the birds in the sky and all the creatures that move along the ground—everything that has the breath of life in it—I give every green plant for food. And it was so" (Genesis 1:29–30).

Wait a minute! Are we really supposed to believe that animals like lions, bears, and crocodiles were vegetarians? As Bible-believing Christians yes, we are. Was Susie's father correct about God designing animals to eat meat? Yes, he was. How can both of these be true? It is really a question about the *timing*. Some animals are well-suited to eat just about anything. Let's take a closer look at bears.

Black bears, grizzly bears, and polar bears all have large sharp teeth and claws but significantly different diets. Bears are omnivorous—they eat both plants and animals and their diets vary depending on what food is available. Black and grizzly bears eat berries, fruit, sedges (grass-like plants), and insects. They will occasionally eat fish, honeycomb, human food, and garbage. Sometimes they prey on young elk and deer or hijack the carcass of animals killed by other predators such as mountain lions.[2,3] On the other hand, polar bears primarily eat seals, walruses, whale carcasses, or even garbage if they live near humans.[4] Why do polar bears eat so much meat? Because it's usually the only available option.

Of course, bears are not the only animals with sharp teeth that will eat plants—certain species of crocodiles do the same thing: Even today, animals use large, sharp teeth to eat plants. One study found that 13 of the 18 crocodilian species it examined eat fruit from 34 different plant families.[5]

Here is the point: God designed these creatures to survive under changing conditions. Before the Fall, bears (and other animals) would have used their teeth and claws to eat just plants. After the Fall they use these same features to eat whatever is available.

God's original creation was indeed very good. Adam and Eve lived in harmony with each other and the animals. They were blessed with the very presence of God himself. What went wrong? Genesis chapter 3 holds the answer to this question.

The Fall (Genesis 3)

When God first placed Adam in the Garden of Eden, He warned Adam not to eat from the tree of knowledge of good and evil:

The LORD God took the man and put him in the Garden of Eden to work it and take care of it. And the LORD God commanded the man, "You are free to eat from any tree in the garden; but you must not eat from the tree of the knowledge of good and evil, for when you eat from it you will certainly die" (Genesis 2:15–17).

This command was a test. It was designed to see if Adam and Eve would faithfully obey God. Unfortunately, even though they lived in paradise, they chose to rebel against Him: "When the woman saw that the fruit of the tree was good for food and pleasing to the eye, and also desirable for gaining wisdom, she took some and ate it. She also gave some to her husband, who was with her, and he ate it" (Genesis 3:6).

What a horrible, tragic event! It is hard to describe the widespread changes Adam and Eve's sin caused! Theologian, author, and pastor John McArthur offered the following comments about the effects of Adam and Eve's rebellion: All the problems of the universe have their origin in the events of this historic account. I'll say that again: all the problems in the universe. Physical problems, spiritual problems, moral problems, social problems, economic problems, political problems, all the problems in the universe have their origin in the events of this historic account.[6] Here are just a few characteristics of life after the Fall:

- There would be strife between men and women (Genesis 3:7,16).
- Women would experience great pain in childbirth (Genesis 3:16).
- The ground was now cursed (Genesis 3:17). We now experience devasting earthquakes, tornados, hurricanes and floods.
- Work would be hard and frustrating (Genesis 3:17–19).
- Death entered the world (Genesis 3:19, Romans 5:12).

- Mankind became very wicked (Genesis 6:5).
- The Earth was filled with violence (Genesis 6:11).
- All of God's beautiful creation was now cursed (Romans 8:21).

Dr. Daniel Biddle, author, speaker and President of Genesis Apologetics, offered the following insight:

> …creation itself is cursed so that it no longer functions properly, which is why we get various natural harms like birth defects, injuries, disease, natural disasters, aging, and death. None of these were according to God's original design. It is because of sin in the world that bad things happen, even to the innocent. We all suffer the effects of the curse, eventually even leading to death for each of us. Romans 5:12 explains that "through one man sin entered the world, and death through sin, and thus death spread to all men, because all sinned." Death is an invader in God's creation because of sin.[7]

When I first learned about the Fall, I was irritated with Adam and Eve. They had everything and blew it! What would everything be like today if they hadn't rebelled? Then I remembered that all of us have sinned against God: "As it is written: There is no one righteous, not even one" (Romans 3:9). Please remember: we no longer live in paradise—we live in a battlefield. Although the world around us still has beauty, our pride and rebellion against God have brought:

- Death
- Disease
- Pain and suffering
- Natural disasters
- Evil

The good news is that we have hope—one day God is going to restore everything! Here are some promises from God:

- "He must remain in heaven until the time comes for God to restore everything, as he promised long ago through his holy prophets" (Acts 3:21).

- "Then I saw a new heaven and a new earth, for the first heaven and the first earth had passed away…" (Revelation 21:1).

- "He who was seated on the throne said, "I am making everything new!" (Revelation 21:5).

- "No longer will there be any curse. The throne of God and of the Lamb will be in the city, and his servants will serve him. They will see his face, and his name will be on their foreheads" (Revelation 22:2–4).

- "And I heard a loud voice from the throne saying, 'Look! God's dwelling place is now among the people, and he will dwell with them. They will be his people, and God himself will be with them and be their God. He will wipe every tear from their eyes. There will be no more death or mourning or crying or pain, for the old order of things has passed away'" (Revelation 21:3–4).

Summary

When we look at the world around us, we still see hints of beauty. However, it is not the same as when God first created it—our sin has corrupted God's once-perfect creation. Although we now live in a battleground, some day we will enjoy living with God in a brand-new Heaven and Earth. In the meantime, let's all do our part by telling others about God's incredible love and offer of forgiveness!

"Father, thank you for loving us. Please forgive us for our sins. Thank you for your incredible offer of forgiveness and eternal life that was bought through your Son, Jesus. We eagerly look forward to the day when we will enjoy living with you in the brand-new Heaven and Earth! In the meantime, please give us the courage and strength we need to live in this fallen world. Amen."

Group Discussion Questions

1. Adam and Eve had everything going for them. They lived in harmony with the animals and each other. They enjoyed the presence of God walking with them in the Garden. Why do you think they chose to rebel against God? Why do you think people rebel today? Please read Genesis Chapter 3 prior to answering.

2. John McArthur and Dr. Biddle both said that sin affects literally everything. Do you agree? How does sin affect:

   - Government?
   - Relationships?
   - Our health?
   - Business?
   - Nature?

3. In the beginning of this chapter, Susie was upset about seeing a lioness attack a zebra and asked her father if God was mean. Assuming Susie is seven years old, what would you tell her?

Chapter 3: Free Will

"But if serving the Lord seems undesirable to you, then choose for yourselves this day whom you will serve...But as for me and my household, we will serve the Lord" (Joshua 24:15).

We all stared at the TV in disbelief: was this really happening? The South Tower of the World Trade Center—one of the tallest buildings in the world—collapsed with a thunderous roar. Scores of people were engulfed by dust and debris as they ran screaming in terror. Earlier that morning, terrorists had hijacked four commercial jetliners. They crashed two of them into the Twin Towers of the World Trade Center and one of them into the Pentagon building. The terrorists planned to crash the fourth plane (United Airlines Flight 93) into the United States Capitol Building, but the passengers and crew bravely fought back causing the plane to crash into the ground. Before that day was over, nearly 3,000 Americans died and countless others were injured. Many people asked "where was God on 9/11?" Why were some people killed and others spared?

These are great questions! However, before we address them, let's back up and talk about creation and the world in which we now live.

In the beginning, God created Adam and Eve. God could have created them as mindless robots that would always obey Him. Instead, He gave Adam and Eve (and us) free will—the option to obey Him or reject Him. God did this even though He knew the full cost of this decision in advance. He knew people would rebel against Him. He knew people would kill and hurt one another. He knew that He would have to send his Son Jesus to die an agonizing death to pay for our sins, *yet He still gave us free will!* Why? It has to do with relationships.

Think about someone you love deeply. Do you love them because you have to or did you choose to love them? Real love requires real choices. Real choices have real consequences. Because mankind chose to rebel against God, we were facing eternity separated from Him. God has real emotions. He loves us and wants us to love Him in return. He wants us to be in Heaven with Him some day. He considers our relationship with Him so important that He chose to give us free will and then send His Son to rescue us from the consequences of our sin: Very rarely will anyone die for a righteous person, though for a good person someone might possibly dare to die. But God demonstrates his own love for us in this: "While we were still sinners, Christ died for us" (Romans 5:7–8).

What an amazing demonstration of love! Now that we have established some context for the world we live in, let's talk about the terrorist attacks of 9/11. Let's start with this: where was God?

He was holding up the Twin Towers long enough to allow thousands of people to escape.

Although the death of nearly 3,000 people is horrific, the death toll could have been much higher. Experts believe there were between 16,400 and 18,000 people in the Twin Towers when they were struck.[8] It is likely the terrorists were hoping to cause the towers to collapse immediately after impact. Instead, the towers remained standing for about an hour after being hit. This allowed time for thousands of people to evacuate. Some experts who reviewed the details of this tragedy said they were amazed the towers did not topple over or collapse sooner. While some people choose to give credit to the original engineers and builders, I personally believe that this was a miracle.

He was turning the hearts of some back to Him.

Tragic events and crisis usually cause people to pause and reflect on their lives—especially their relationships. The horrible events of 9/11 caused some people to think about their relationship with God and make some changes—people like the Stanton family:

> Yet out of all this darkness around Ground Zero came a guiding light. The terrorists were shouting "God is Great!" as they crashed into the Twin Towers. But what they were really doing was a horrific act for Satan. Still, even in that horror, the One True God was able to bring good.

In the case of the Stantons, having stared death in the face where the Towers once stood, they now realized they wanted a real relationship with the God of life and were totally dependent on Him for their future. They repented of their past. "I'd let Jesus out of a box on a Sunday and then I'd go back to my life on the weekdays. Pretty much everything I was doing was all chasing after a whim," Christina confessed. "It was just the realization that I'd been living my life really without God."[9]

He was using circumstances to prevent some people from being there when the planes hit.

After 9/11, many people shared stories about why they were not in the World Trade Center during the attack. These stories include car trouble, traffic accidents, illnesses, surprise visits from relatives, breaking up with a fiancée, sick children and getting laid off from a job. Some people might attribute these stories to coincidence or luck, but I believe that God used them to save certain people that day. You can read some of these stories at: 9/11 Survivor Stories: Twists of Fate That Saved These People's Lives.[10]

He was welcoming some of His children into Heaven.

So why were some people killed and others spared? Honestly this question can only be answered by God himself.

Unfortunately, some Christians mistakenly believe that the people who perished during the 9/11 attacks (and other disasters) were being punished by God. However, the Bible teaches us that this is often not the case. Please consider the following.

During Jesus's earthly ministry, many people believed that those who perished were somehow targeted by God. Jesus reminded them (and us) that all people are guilty of sinning and need to repent:

> Now there were some present at that time who
> told Jesus about the Galileans whose blood
> Pilate had mixed with their sacrifices. Jesus
> answered, "Do you think that these Galileans
> were worse sinners than all the other Galileans
> because they suffered this way? I tell you, no!
> But unless you repent, you too will all perish. Or
> those eighteen who died when the tower in
> Siloam fell on them—do you think they were
> more guilty than all the others living in
> Jerusalem? I tell you, no! But unless you
> repent, you too will all perish (Luke 13:1–5).

According to the book of Isaiah, sometimes God takes righteous people home to spare them from evil:

> The righteous perish, and no one takes it to heart;
> the devout are taken away, and no one
> understands that the righteous are taken away to
> be spared from evil. Those who walk uprightly
> enter into peace; they find rest as they lie in
> death (Isaiah 57:1–3).

Sometimes God takes righteous people home without giving us the reason: "Altogether, Enoch lived a total of 365 years. Enoch walked faithfully with God; then he was no more, because God took him away" (Genesis 5:23–24).

Here is another example:

> As they were walking along and talking together,
> suddenly a chariot of fire and horses of fire
> appeared and separated the two of them, and
> Elijah went up to heaven in a whirlwind. Elisha
> saw this and cried out, "My father! My father!
> The chariots and horsemen of Israel!" And
> Elisha saw him no more. Then he took hold of
> his garment and tore it in two (2 Kings 2:11–12).

The bottom line is that we usually do not (and often cannot) know why God allows certain people to perish while saving others. Please remember that God has perfect knowledge and sees the whole picture:

> For my thoughts are not your thoughts, neither
> are your ways my ways," declares the Lord. "As
> the heavens are higher than the earth, so are my
> ways higher than your ways and my thoughts
> than your thoughts (Isaiah 55:7–8).

As we have seen, God has given mankind the gift of free will. Unfortunately, some people choose to reject God and engage in acts of unspeakable evil. So, is there anything we can do about it? Yes! Here are some suggestions:

Hate evil and overcome it by doing good!

- Refrain from doing evil ourselves: "Love must be sincere. Hate what is evil; cling to what is good" (Romans 12:9).

- "…keep your tongue from evil and your lips from telling lies. Turn from evil and do good; seek peace and pursue it" (Psalm 34:13–14).

- If you see something evil happening do something about it right away! Personally, I hate to hear news stories about someone being attacked while bystanders did nothing to help. When someone asks me "Why doesn't God do something to help them?" my response is "What have **you** done to help? Maybe God sent you to help out." Moses set a great example for us to follow: "Now a priest of Midian had seven daughters, and they came to draw water and fill the troughs to water their father's flock. Some shepherds came along and drove them away, but Moses got up and came to their rescue and watered their flock" (Exodus 2:16–17).

- The parable of the Good Samaritan is another great example: "In reply Jesus said: A man was going down from Jerusalem to Jericho, when he was attacked by robbers. They stripped him of his clothes, beat him and went away, leaving him half dead. A priest happened to be going down the same road, and when he saw the man, he passed by on the other side. So too, a Levite, when he came to the place and saw him, passed by on the other side. But a Samaritan, as he traveled, came where the man was; and when he saw him, he took pity on him. He went to him and bandaged his wounds, pouring on oil and wine. Then he put the man on his own donkey, brought him to an inn and took care of him. The next day he took out two denarii and gave them to the innkeeper. 'Look after him,' he said, 'and when I return, I will reimburse you for any extra expense you may have" (Luke 10:30–35).

- Donate your time, talent and money to organizations that help the poor, fight against evil or help the victims of violent crimes.

- "Do not be overcome by evil, but overcome evil with good" (Romans 12:21).

- Elect officials who will ensure that criminals are brought to justice (please note I am **not** advocating voting for one political party verses the other!).

- "It is not good to be partial to the wicked and so deprive the innocent of justice" (Proverbs 18:5).

Remember that God is just and will eventually punish the wicked

- "Do not repay anyone evil for evil. Be careful to do what is right in the eyes of everyone" (Romans 12:17).

- "Do not be deceived: God cannot be mocked. A man reaps what he sows" (Galatians 6:7).

- "It is mine to avenge; I will repay. In due time their foot will slip; their day of disaster is near and their doom rushes upon them" (Deuteronomy 32:35).

- "Do not be amazed at this, for a time is coming when all who are in their graves will hear his voice and come out—those who have done what is good will rise to live, and those who have done what is evil will rise to be condemned" (John 5:28–30).

- Even the devil and his angels will be punished: "Then he will say to those on his left, 'Depart from me, you who are cursed, into the eternal fire prepared for the devil and his angels'" (Matthew 25:41).

Summary

God created humans and angels with free will—the ability to choose to love or reject Him. Although God knew this decision would ultimately cause a lot of pain and suffering, He did it anyway because true relationships require choice. God will eventually punish Satan, demons and wicked people—they will not get away with their evil deeds! In the meantime, we should abstain from doing evil ourselves and do everything in our power to fight against it and help those hurt by it.

"Lord, it is so hard to see evil happening in this world. We know that you see all things and will eventually punish the wicked. Until that day, please use us to fight against evil and help those who are hurting. Amen."

Group Discussion Questions

1. Did anything in this chapter surprise you? If so, what was it?

2. Have you, or someone you know, assumed that people who are the victims of terrorism or natural disasters were being punished by God? Do you still feel the same way?

3. What are some practical ways that we can fight against evil and help those who have been victimized?

Chapter 4: Spiritual Warfare

"Be alert and of sober mind. Your enemy the devil prowls around like a roaring lion looking for someone to devour. Resist him, standing firm in the faith, because you know that the family of believers throughout the world is undergoing the same kind of sufferings" (1 Peter 5:7–9).

"Almost there!" Dan thought as he made the final connections. It was going to be an interesting night. He was giving a presentation in a new location and was struggling to connect his laptop to the church's audio-visual equipment. "What will God do tonight?" Dan wondered. At that point Dan heard a commotion. He took a deep breath and headed outside. The man in the parking lot was out of control! He was screaming at one of the church elders and was so upset, he wasn't even finishing his own sentences. The problem? The church had the audacity to invite Genesis Apologetics to come speak. The situation was growing worse and it looked like violence was imminent. Dan went to his truck and retrieved his pepper spray preparing for the worst. At this point, another man from the church arrived. He recognized what was happening and said "Let's pray."

They prayed in the name of Jesus against the demon that was manifesting. Specifically, they prayed to bind and silence it. They were far enough away that the man couldn't hear them but the demon did! Soon after they started praying, the angry man suddenly stopped screaming, got into his vehicle, and left. Dan and the two church elders praised God and headed into the church.

Many people (including Christians) focus too much on the physical world around us and forget that we are living in the middle of a fierce spiritual battle. Apparently, humans are not the only ones that God gave free will. We have some unseen, powerful enemies who are intent upon our destruction—Satan and his demons. The Bible has a lot to say about them:

- "Be alert and of sober mind. Your enemy the devil prowls around like a roaring lion looking for someone to devour" (1 Peter 5:8).

- "The thief comes only to steal and kill and destroy. I came that they may have life and have it abundantly" (John 10:9–11, ESV).

- "You are of your father the devil, and your will is to do your father's desires. He was a murderer from the beginning, and does not stand in the truth, because there is no truth in him. When he lies, he speaks out of his own character, for he is a liar and the father of lies" (John 8:44, ESV).

Satan hates God and wants to hurt Him. He is smart and knows that the best way to hurt God is to hurt His favorite creation—people. Satan's ultimate goal is to forever separate as many people from God as possible. To accomplish his goal, he and his demons use a variety of tactics including distractions (Acts 16:16–18), false doctrines (1 Timothy 4:1), deception (2 Corinthians 11:2–4), lies (John 8:44), planting seeds of doubt (Genesis 3:1), fear, physical oppression (Acts 19:13–16) and demonic possession (Matthew 4:24).

Jesus confronted and expelled several demons. So did the disciples and Paul the Apostle. Although some people think that demons were only present during "Biblical times," they are still present today! Although I usually don't talk about it, during the past 20 years of ministry I have personally encountered demons on several occasions. They can be frightening! In this next section are some suggestions that may help.

Accept Christ

If you have never accepted Jesus as your Lord and Savior, considering doing so today. Satan and his demons are no match for Jesus Christ! The Bible tells us that Satan and his demons have been defeated and are headed for destruction:

- "I have told you these things, so that in me you may have peace. In this world you will have trouble. But take heart! I have overcome the world" (John 16:33).

- "You, dear children, are from God and have overcome them, because the one who is in you is greater than the one who is in the world" (John 16:32–33).

- "Then he will say to those on his left, 'Depart from me, you who are cursed, into the eternal fire prepared for the devil and his angels" (Matthew 25:41).

Pray on the Full Armor of God

There is an old adage that says "if the Devil isn't bothering you, you're not bothering him." In other words, if you are serving Jesus Christ, expect opposition here on Earth. Be prepared and put on the full armor of God:

> Finally, be strong in the Lord and in his mighty power. Put on the full armor of God, so that you can take your stand against the devil's schemes. For our struggle is not against flesh and blood, but against the rulers, against the authorities, against the powers of this dark world and against the spiritual forces of evil in the heavenly realms" (Ephesians 6:10–12).

Realize That the Battle is for Our Minds

> Therefore, I urge you, brothers and sisters, in
> view of God's mercy, to offer your bodies as a
> living sacrifice, holy and pleasing to God—this
> is your true and proper worship. Do not conform
> to the pattern of this world, but be transformed
> by the renewing of your mind. Then you will be
> able to test and approve what God's will is—his
> good, pleasing and perfect will" (Romans 12:1–
> 3).

Let Go of Bitterness and Rage

Do not harbor anger in your heart: "In your anger do not
sin": Do not let the sun go down while you are still angry, and
do not give the devil a foothold" (Ephesians 4:26–27).

Remember that some people, like the man mentioned in
the story earlier, may not even be aware they are being used by
Satan:

> Opponents must be gently instructed, in the hope
> that God will grant them repentance leading
> them to a knowledge of the truth, and that they
> will come to their senses and escape from the
> trap of the devil, who has taken them captive to
> do his will" (2 Timothy 2:25–26).

Maintain a Balanced Perspective

Be aware that demons exist, but don't over spiritualize
everything. We should not look for a demon under every bush.
Although demons can cause physical impairment, colds, flu,
cancer, birth defects, and other maladies, these problems are
usually a consequence of living in our fallen world.

Close the Gateways

Avoid videos, TV shows, movies, websites, video games, magazines and activities that include witchcraft, violence or pornography. These provide gateways to your heart:

Finally, brothers and sisters, whatever is true, whatever is noble, whatever is right, whatever is pure, whatever is lovely, whatever is admirable—if anything is excellent or praiseworthy—think about such things. Whatever you have learned or received or heard from me, or seen in me—put it into practice. And the God of peace will be with you" (Philippians 4:7–9).

The acts of the flesh are obvious: sexual immorality, impurity and debauchery; idolatry and witchcraft; hatred, discord, jealousy, fits of rage, selfish ambition, dissensions, factions and envy; drunkenness, orgies, and the like. I warn you, as I did before, that those who live like this will not inherit the kingdom of God" (Galatians 5:19–21).

Summary

There is an unseen battle going on all around us. It is a battle for the hearts, minds and souls of people. Satan and his demons want to destroy us (John 10:10) and will use any means possible to accomplish their goal. Although we cannot usually see spiritual combat, we can easily see the effects it has upon the world around us. As Christians, we need to guard our hearts and minds and put on the full armor of God each and every day. Even though some days will be dark, we should rejoice in the knowledge that God wins in the end.

Group Discussion Questions

1. Some people believe that demons are not real yet the Bible is very clear about their existence. Have you ever encountered someone who is being oppressed or controlled by a demon? Have you ever sought help from your church only to be told that demons do not really exist? Briefly share your experiences with the other people in your group.

2. Do you think Christians should avoid watching movies that feature witchcraft (e.g., Harry Potter)? Why or why not? You may want to watch our free video on this topic: Should Christians Watch Movies Like Harry Potter? It is available at: _www.youtube.com/watch?v=yazllYgW1Qk_

3. Read Ephesians 6:10–17. What are some practical ways Christians can put on the "full armor of God" every day?

Chapter 5: Bad Choices & Decisions

"A person's own folly leads to their ruin, yet their heart rages against the LORD" (Proverbs 19:3).

It happened in a heartbeat. One moment I was installing wiring and the next I was on the ground writhing in pain. My lower back felt like it was on fire and I could no longer feel my legs. As I laid there, I noticed a battered chainsaw on the ground next to me. The chainsaw had fallen from the trusses of the house (about 12 feet) and hit me in the back. Apparently, someone had left the chainsaw balanced in a truss and then left the jobsite. What was I going to do? There were no cell phones back then and no one else was working at the site. I was quite alone. After about 20 minutes, the feeling in my legs began to return and I managed to stagger outside and flag someone down for help. I didn't know it then but what happened next would affect me for the rest of my life.

The first one I called for help was my boss. He was upset, but not for the reason you might think. He did not want to report another accident because it would increase the cost of his worker's compensation insurance. Unfortunately, I had no healthcare at the time because I could not afford it but made too much money to qualify for government programs. My boss convinced me not to seek medical attention and take a few paid days off instead. The result? A twisted back and a lifetime of pain.

There is not a single day I don't experience some level of pain. Some days it is a minor inconvenience while other days I can barely get out of bed. I have been examined by chiropractors, doctors, and physical therapists. They all say basically the same thing: "If only you had sought treatment right after that accident!"

So here is the million-dollar question: Is my back pain God's fault? I would say no. Consider the following:

- This accident was caused by someone else's bad decision. Of course, God could have prevented it, but chose to let it happen. Perhaps He allowed it to teach me to rely on Him in my weakness and/or keep me humble. It reminds me of when Paul asked God three times to remove the "thorn in the flesh" (2 Corinthians 12:6–8) but God refused to do so.

- I let my boss convince me not to seek proper medical attention through Workers' Compensation. Although I didn't have heath care coverage, I could have sued the company responsible for my injury but chose not to do this. According to medical experts, my injuries were treatable right after the accident. Therefore, my back pain today is (at least in part) a consequence of my poor decisions.

- If the chainsaw had hit me in the head, it would have killed me instantly because I was not wearing a hardhat. I am truly grateful that didn't happen because I was not saved at the time!

Over the years, I have made many mistakes and suffered from various types of injuries so I am well acquainted with living with pain. I would love to tell you that I have always endured it with a smile but that would not be the truth.

In 2010 I injured my ankle in a poolside accident. Although I went to the doctor a total of six times, they told me that it was just a sprain and that my back was likely the real problem. At times my ankle felt like it was on fire! There were times when I literally blacked out from pain. For two years I limped around and sank into the depths of depression.

Sometimes the pain was so overwhelming that I literally prayed for God to end my life. I didn't just ask Him—I yelled, begged and even taunted Him. I'm not proud of this, but living with constant pain is very challenging!

After two years I changed healthcare plans and discovered the truth: one of the ligaments in my ankle had torn off with pieces of bone still attached to it. There were several shards of bone in my ankle and one of them was pressing on a nerve. The surgeon who examined and repaired my ankle expressed his amazement (and disgust) at the negligence of my previous doctors. After a lengthy recovery process, I'm happy to report my ankle is now much better.

Emotional Pain

Of course, physical pain is only one type of suffering. Many of us suffer from deep emotional wounds caused by our own mistakes or other people's decisions. Emotional suffering can be far worse than physical pain. We feel the pain of broken relationships, rejection, betrayal, neglect, abandonment or abuse. Depression can feel like falling into a deep pit of quicksand with no way out. To make matters worse, Satan and his demons often whisper lies to us to keep us isolated and discouraged. So, what can we do about it? After suffering from depression for many years, my advice is to seek professional, Godly counseling as soon as possible!

If you own a car (especially a newer model), you know how incredibly complicated they are. When trouble comes, we need to seek the services of a qualified mechanic. The same is true about us—we really are "fearfully and wonderfully made" (Psalm 139:14). When we are struggling with anger, emotional pain, bitterness and/or depression, we need to seek help from a professional. Although having trusted friends is wonderful, they are not a good substitute for professional counseling. Please do not let pride stop you from getting help!

A good counselor will help you sort out your emotions and develop a pathway to help you heal. One note of caution: it is extremely important to make sure that the counselor you choose has a Biblical worldview!

Summary

Everyone makes mistakes. Sometimes we get away with bad decisions while others lead to horrible consequences. However, when this happens, we should humbly accept responsibility for our actions and not blame the Lord. Sometimes other people make bad decisions that harm us.

When this occurs, it is easy for us to blame God and doubt His goodness. Living with chronic physical or emotional pain often leads to deep depression. When this happens, we need to seek help from a professional counselor who has a Biblical worldview. Please do not give up! One day we will enjoy our new bodies and live in Heaven with God!

"Lord Jesus, you know first-hand what it feels like to suffer severe physical and emotional pain. Thank you for taking our place on the cross and conquering death so that we can someday live with you in Heaven. It will be so wonderful living without any more tears, sorrow, pain or death! In the meantime, please be with us and send Godly people to help us during our struggles. We love you! Amen."

Group Discussion Questions

1. Have you ever been seriously injured by a mistake you made? Did you blame God or someone else when it happened? Briefly share your experience with the others in your group.

2. Have you ever been seriously injured by someone else? Have you been able to forgive them yet? If so, please share your experience.

3. Have you ever suffered from depression? Did you recover from it? If so, what advice would you offer to people who are still suffering?

Chapter 6: Test & Grow Our Faith

"Consider it pure joy, my brothers and sisters, whenever you face trials of many kinds, because you know that the testing of your faith produces perseverance" (James 1:2–3).

It was raining hard that night. The weather forecast called for 2–3 inches of rain and many of the local streets were flooded. I wasn't feeling well and was grateful that I didn't have to go anywhere. Then the phone rang. It was the care facility: my mother had contracted pneumonia and wasn't expected to make it through the night. After talking and praying about it with my wife, I felt like God was leading me to go.

On the ride to the care facility, I thought about my relationship with my mother. Two years before she was full of life and fun to be around (unless she was drinking). All of that changed when she fell off a curb and injured her neck. Shortly after that, she became addicted to pain killers. Despite our family's best efforts to intervene, she destroyed herself and ended up with dementia in a care facility.

My relationship with my mother was complicated. When she was sober, she was fun, loving and a great mother. However, when she got drunk (which was often), she was full of hate and was verbally abusive. My thoughts were interrupted by our arrival at the care facility—it was time to say goodbye to my mother.

When I saw my mother, I was shocked. She looked so weak and helpless. She was sedated and breathing oxygen through a mask. Her breathing was raspy and her body burned with fever. As I held her hand, I wept quietly and asked her to forgive me for my part in our strained relationship. I knew my mother was not a Christian and was suffering from alcohol and drug-induced dementia. I asked God to reach into her diseased mind and save her soul. After praying for a few moments, I clearly heard the Lord tell me "I've got this." I kissed my mother on the forehead and left. That was the last time I saw

her. Will I see her in Heaven some day? I sure hope so but I
trust God to do the right thing: "The Lord is not slow in
keeping his promise, as some understand slowness. Instead he
is patient with you, not wanting anyone to perish, but everyone
to come to repentance" (2 Peter 3:9).

To be completely honest, my first reaction when I read James telling us to consider trials as "pure joy (James 1:2–3) is to yell at him. Are you kidding me James? How in the world am I supposed to do that? Although the death of my mother was painful, this was just one of many challenges I faced in 2017. Below are a few more.

During the summer of 2017, I agreed to help teach creation at an eight-week summer school program. My role included teaching, developing the curriculum, games and activities for over 500 students. Since I was still working a full-time secular job and attending college courses at night, this proved to be quite the challenge!

Before summer camp began, I noticed a small sore on my lower lip that did not seem to healing properly. When I visited my doctor, he seemed very concerned and scheduled a biopsy. The results of the biopsy indicated that I had a common form of skin cancer called squamous cell carcinoma. The problem was the cancer was actually under the first layer of skin and was much larger than the sore indicated. Surgery was scheduled for two weeks after summer camp ended.

The surgical procedures included removal of the cancerous cells followed by repair and reconstruction. The first part was extremely painful. The surgeon had to remove around 25% of my lower lip. To make matters worse, the anesthesia started to wear off after about 30 minutes. The pain was excruciating! All I could do was grip the edges of the chair and try not to yell out.

The reconstructive phase of the surgery was initially much less painful. However, in order to access enough material to replace the missing part of my lip, the surgeon had to cut a slit from my mouth down to the lower part of my chin.

During my recovery period, I wondered if I would ever be able to teach again. My lip was so swollen and parts of my face were numb for weeks after the surgery. Because of this, I was unable to speak clearly and had a nasty scar running from my mouth down to my chin.

At that time, we had a wonderful toy schnauzer named Rosie. Our little dog was about 10 years old and had been a source of comfort for my wife and I during hard times. During the second week of my recovery, Rosie was diagnosed with cancer. Her whole abdominal cavity was filled with tumors and she had to be put down immediately.

It would be great to tell you that these events did not impact my faith but that simply would not be the truth. During the latter part of 2017, I experienced a major crisis of faith that was so intense I almost walked away from God. I never doubted God's power—I doubted His goodness and love. Unfortunately, knowing a bunch of theology and Bible verses provided absolutely no comfort to me during that time! It was the love, patience and concern of my wife and a few close friends that brought me back from the brink.

If you have attended church for any length of time, you are probably familiar with Romans 8:28: "And we know that God causes everything to work together for the good of those who love God and are called according to his purpose for them."

In this passage, God promises to use all things (good, bad and ugly) for our good. Please note that this promise only applies to Christians! Otherwise, bad things are just bad things. Looking back in my life, I now see the truth of this passage. It is encouraging to see that God is always at work for us, fighting on our behalf through all of our difficult circumstances. Here are some positive outcomes from my challenging experiences:

1. I can relate and minister to children who have a mother who is an alcoholic.

2. I now have empathy for others who have lost a parent to drug addiction.

3. I have experienced a small taste of what is it like to have cancer and the fear of reoccurrence.

4. I realize more than ever how blessed I am to have my wife and best friends—they are amazing people!

5. My faith is stronger than it was before.

6. I know from experience that God truly does work all things for the good of those who love Him.

Summary

It's easy to trust God when things are going well, but trusting Him during the storms of life is much harder! Jesus said that His followers would experience trouble (John 16:33) but promised to use "all things" for our good (Romans 8:28). Trials can increase our faith but they can also create a spiritual crisis. It is important to have Godly people alongside you to help you get through the tough times.

"Lord, thank you for promising to use all things for our good! Please comfort and guide us during the trials of life. Please use these trials to strengthen us and prepare us to minister to others who are experiencing suffering. Amen."

Group Discussion Questions

1. Why do you think it is so hard for some of us to trust God during trials?

2. Have you ever looked back at a dark period of your life and realized that God somehow used it to grow your faith? Sometimes God takes a long time to answer our

prayers. Because of this, some people find it very encouraging to keep a journal of answered prayers.

3. Have you been able to comfort someone because you have been through similar circumstances?

Chapter 7: Discipline and Punishment

"Know then in your heart that as a man disciplines his son, so the LORD your God disciplines you" (Deuteronomy 8:5).

It was late in the evening. It had been a rough night—the kids were challenging and had made a huge mess. All of the helpers had left so I was on my own. To make matters worse, my back was hurting so badly I had to crawl along the floor to pick up the astonishing collection of trash that was strewn everywhere. As the tears welled up in my eyes, I was feeling quite sorry for myself. I asked myself again why I had agreed to teach these kids.

After collecting all of the trash, I made my way to the dumpster. The light near the dumpster wasn't working, so I failed to notice the board lying in wait for me. You guessed it—I tripped over the board and spilled the trash that I had worked so hard to collect. At that point I completely lost it! I literally yelled at God. I accused Him of being heartless and cruel and announced that I was done serving Him. In the middle of my rant a door across the courtyard opened and one of the pastors stuck his head out. My heart sank—did he hear my rant? "Dave," he said, "Make sure you turn off the lights—you left them on last week." Unbelievable. As I stood there fuming, I asked God why He was being so unkind—after all we were on the same team...right?

At that point, I felt like God quietly asked me a question: "If you are truly on my team then why haven't you obeyed me?" Ouch! I immediately knew what He was talking about. About nine months earlier, God had put it on my heart to start a creation ministry. Instead, I transferred to another church. I had made the same mistake as Jonah and was now experiencing God's hand of discipline.

In the book of Jonah, God told Jonah to go to Nineveh and deliver a message to the Assyrians: repent now or be destroyed. But Jonah refused to go. Instead, he booked passage on a ship bound for Tarshish—the opposite direction of Nineveh. God used a fierce storm and a giant fish to change Jonah's mind. Ultimately, Jonah delivered the message, but he still had a hard heart towards the Assyrians. Jonah did not want the Assyrians to repent and be saved, he wanted God to destroy them because they were cruel, awful people.

The reason that I initially refused to obey God was very different than Jonah's. I didn't want to start a creation ministry because I didn't trust God enough. I can tell you from experience that serving in a creation ministry is not for the faint-hearted. People engaged in creation ministry endure a lot of persecution! We have been slandered, rejected, mocked, falsely accused and "cancelled" by people we know and love. Believe it or not, we have even received death threats. Is it worth it?

Although I sometimes struggle with discouragement, occasionally we receive feedback from people that show that the Lord is busy restoring hearts and minds through our ministry. It is amazing to watch kids smile as they learn about dinosaurs from a Biblical perspective. It is amazing to see the relief on the faces of high school students when they learn that God did indeed create everything and they did not evolve from ape-like creatures. It's amazing to see how adults' lives change once they realize they can trust the whole Bible—not just the New Testament. At this point, I have been blessed with the opportunity to teach thousands of students and adults! Yes, it is definitely worth it, but I almost missed out on all of this because of my disobedience.

If you are a parent, you know that disciplining your child is unpleasant yet necessary. As parents we love our children and want the best for them. Disciplining our children helps shape their character and teach them right from wrong. The same is true about our Heavenly Father. He rebukes and disciplines us for our own good:

> If you are not disciplined—and everyone
> undergoes discipline—then you are not
> legitimate, not true sons and daughters at all.

Moreover, we have all had human fathers who disciplined us and we respected them for it. How much more should we submit to the Father of spirits and live! They disciplined us for a little while as they thought best; but God disciplines us for our good, in order that we may share in his holiness (Hebrews 12:8–10).

Blessed is the one whom God corrects; so do not despise the discipline of the Almighty. For he wounds, but he also binds up; he injures, but his hands also heal (Job 5:17–18).

My son, do not despise the Lord's discipline, and do not resent his rebuke, because the Lord disciplines those he loves, as a father the son he delights in (Proverbs 3:11–12).

Although experiencing God's discipline is never fun, He does it to shape our character and steer us in the right direction. If you are experiencing hardship, please spend some time with God and ask Him to reveal any rebellion or disobedience in your heart. Of course, there are plenty of other reasons for suffering, but don't be like Jonah and make God send a great fish after you to get your attention!

Summary

Like any good parent, our heavenly Father disciplines us when we ignore His instructions. Although being disciplined is unpleasant, God uses it to teach us to obey Him and trust that His way is better than ours. When we choose to disobey God, we may miss out on the opportunities and blessings that come from walking in obedience.

"Father God, thank you for loving us enough to discipline us when we go astray. Please help us learn to listen more closely to you and trust you enough to obey you. Amen."

Group Discussion Questions

1. When you were a child, how did you feel about being disciplined?

2. As an adult, has your perspective about discipline changed at all? If so, how has it changed?

3. Have you ever been disciplined by God for not obeying Him? What happened? What advice would you offer to others?

Chapter 8: God's Purpose

"As he went along, he saw a man blind from birth. His disciples asked him, "Rabbi, who sinned, this man or his parents, that he was born blind?" "Neither this man nor his parents sinned," said Jesus, "but this happened so that the works of God might be displayed in him" (John 9:1–3).

The couple stared down at their baby in shock. "Why Lord?" the father asked. Their son had no arms or legs—only a foot-like appendage where one of his legs should be. His mother had three sonograms during her pregnancy, yet none of them had indicated any problems. The doctors said that could not find any medical reason why Nick was born this way. What they didn't realize was that God had great plans for Nick—he was going to be one of the greatest evangelists of all time!

So far in our journey, we have covered six reasons why bad things happen. This last reason has been the hardest one for me to accept. Let's start with the blind man mentioned in John 9:1–3.

The man that Jesus healed was born blind. When the disciples asked Jesus about the cause of the man's blindness, Jesus told them it was so that He could heal the man on that day (I am aware that some theologians interpret this section of scripture differently but it seems pretty straight forward to me). Think about the implications: God caused this man to be born blind and let him struggle for years so that Jesus could heal him? Wow! On the surface that seems so unfair, but if we back up and look deeper, there is more going on in this story that meets the eye. Let's take a look at what happened before and after this miracle:

- Before this miracle occurred, Jesus was in Jerusalem and taught the crowds during the Festival of Tabernacles (John 7:14–24).

- There was a lot of debate and division amongst the Jews about the real identity of Jesus (John 7:25–44).

- In John chapter 8, Jesus had a heated confrontation with the Pharisees. During this confrontation, Jesus identified Himself as God (John 8:58). At this point the Pharisees picked up stones to kill Him but Jesus hid himself and slipped away (John 8:59).

- Jesus healed the blind man (John 9:1–3).

- The Jewish leaders investigated and tried to discredit the miracle (John 9:13–34).

- The man that Jesus healed acknowledged Jesus as the Messiah (John 9:35–39).

This miracle served a special purpose—it provided proof to many people that Jesus was indeed the Son of God. Because of this, the blind man placed his faith in Jesus. Although it is true the blind man suffered until being healed, he received much more than just his physical sight—he received eternal life! Undoubtedly many others who directly witnessed or heard about this miracle also placed their trust in Jesus. It has been nearly two thousand years since this miracle took place and we are still reading and talking about it! The bottom line: God cares more about our eternal destination than our comfort here on Earth. Let's look at a modern-day example.

Nick Vujicic was born in 1982 without arms or legs—he only had a "flipper-like" appendage where one of his legs should be. Everyone was very surprised—the three sonograms his mother had during her pregnancy had not revealed any problems and the doctors could not find any medical reason for Nick's condition. According to Nick's biography, the early years of his life were extremely challenging:

The early days were difficult. Throughout his childhood, Nick not only dealt with the typical challenges of school and adolescence, but he also struggled with depression and loneliness. Nick constantly wondered why he was different than all the other kids. He questioned the purpose of life, or if he even had a purpose.[11]

In 2001, Nick had his first public speaking engagement. He was only 19 years old at that time. In 2005, Nick moved from Australia to California and founded the Life Without Limbs (LWL) ministry. Over the years, Nick Vujicic has inspired and shared the gospel with millions of people. In fact, over *one million people* have made a decision for Christ through LWL ministries! Although Nick has no arms or legs, God is using him in a mighty way! So how did Nick overcome his struggles?

Here is his secret: According to Nick, the victory over his struggles, as well as his strength and passion for life today, can be credited to his faith in God. His family, friends and the many people he has encountered along the journey have inspired him to carry on.[12]

Years ago, I had the chance to meet Nick when he spoke at our church. When I think about his story, I am so humbled. Nick could have chosen to be mad at God for his condition. Instead, he has an amazing attitude and he loves God with all of his heart! Nick is a gifted speaker and has a great sense of humor. He has traveled all over the world sharing the gospel. My physical pain pales in comparison to the everyday challenges he faces. Nick Vujicic's story has inspired me to keep going. Perhaps his story will encourage you as well. Please check out the Life Without Limbs ministry at *www.lifewithoutlimbs.org*.

Summary

Sometimes God uses our physical challenges and harsh circumstances to lead people to Him. Since our lives are so short in comparison to eternity, our comfort is not God's priority—it is to save our souls. We have a choice to make: we can choose to be mad at God about our situation, or we can be like Nick and choose to serve Him: "If God can use a man without arms and legs to be His hands and feet, then He will certainly use any willing heart!"[10]

Pastor Charles (Chuck) Swindoll wrote an incredible poem about the importance of attitude:

> The longer I live, the more I realize the impact of attitude on life. Attitude, to me, is more important than facts. It is more important than the past, than education, than money, than circumstances, than failures, than successes, than what other people think, say or do. It is more important than appearance, giftedness or skill. It will make or break a company... a church... a home. The remarkable thing is we have a choice every day regarding the attitude we embrace for that day. We cannot change our past... we cannot change the fact that people will act in a certain way. We cannot change the inevitable. The only thing we can do is play the one string we have, and that is our attitude...I am convinced that life is 10% what happens to me and 90% how I react to it.[13]

"Dear Lord, please help us not to be angry with you regarding our circumstances. Please help us see the bigger picture—the things that You are working out for the sake of us and others. Holy Spirit please fill us so that we can serve You with passion like Nick Vujicic! Amen."

Group Discussion Questions

1. Do you think the man born blind and/or Nick Vujicic have a right to be angry at God? Why or why not?

2. According to Chuck Swindoll, "life is 10% what happens to us and 90% how we react to it." Do you agree with this statement? Why or why not?

3. Why do you think it is important for us to try to see things from an eternal perspective?

Chapter 9: Conclusion

During our journey, we have explored seven reasons why bad things happen to good people. We have discovered people and Satan are responsible for most of the pain and suffering we see in this world. We have learned that God sometimes uses pain and suffering to discipline us when we go astray. We also learned that sometimes God deliberately creates people with disabilities and uses them to lead people to salvation.

The Bible is filled with God's promises to us. When times get tough, it may be helpful to remember these four:

1. God will eventually punish the wicked:

    -   "Do not be deceived: God cannot be mocked. A man reaps what he sows" (Galatians 6:7).

    -   "Do not be amazed at this, for a time is coming when all who are in their graves will hear his voice and come out—those who have done what is good will rise to live, and those who have done what is evil will rise to be condemned" (John 5:28–30).

2. God will always be by your side: "It is the Lord who goes before you. He will be with you; he will not leave you or forsake you. Do not fear or be dismayed" (Deuteronomy 31:8).

3. God will work all things for the good of those who love Him: "And we know that God causes everything to work together for the good of those who love God and are called according to his purpose for them" (Romans 8:28).

4. Someday we will be with God forever in a new heaven and earth: "And I heard a loud voice from the throne saying, "Look! God's dwelling place is now among the people, and he will dwell with them. They will be his people, and God himself will be with them and be their God. He will wipe every tear from their eyes. There will be no more death or mourning or crying or pain, for the old order of things has passed away" (Revelation 21:3–4).

The Christian life is a marathon not a sprint. God never intended for us to run this race alone! Let's do our best to stay focused and finish the race set before us:

Therefore, since we are surrounded by such a great cloud of witnesses, let us throw off everything that hinders and the sin that so easily entangles. And let us run with perseverance the race marked out for us, fixing our eyes on Jesus, the pioneer and perfecter of faith. For the joy set before him he endured the cross, scorning its shame, and sat down at the right hand of the throne of God. Consider him who endured such opposition from sinners, so that you will not grow weary and lose heart (Hebrews 12:1–3).

It is my sincere hope that this book has helped strengthen your faith and provided some level of comfort. During dark times, please remember that the evil around us is not God's fault. God loves us and because of Jesus's incredible sacrifice, believers will one day spend the rest of eternity with God in paradise! Remember that no matter how dark things may get, God wins in the end!

Practical Exercise

Please read each of the following passages in the Bible and then decide which of the seven categories apply to that situation. Briefly explain the reason for your answer. **Hint: there may be more than one correct answer.**

1. Read Job 1:1–22

☐ Fallen World   ☐ Free Will
☐ Spiritual Warfare   ☐ Bad Choices/Decisions
☐ Punishment / Discipline ☐ Test / Grow Our Faith
☐ God's Purpose

Reasons:

_____

_____

_____

_____

_____

2. Read Jonah 1:1–16

☐ Fallen World   ☐ Free Will
☐ Spiritual Warfare   ☐ Bad Choices/Decisions
☐ Punishment / Discipline ☐ Test / Grow Our Faith
☐ God's Purpose

Reasons:

_____

_____

_____

_____

_____

3. Read Acts 5:1–11

☐ Fallen World   ☐ Free Will
☐ Spiritual Warfare   ☐ Bad Choices/Decisions
☐ Punishment / Discipline   ☐ Test / Grow Our Faith
☐ God's Purpose

Reasons:

_____

_____

_____

_____

_____

4. Read Matthew 4:24

☐ Fallen World   ☐ Free Will
☐ Spiritual Warfare   ☐ Bad Choices/Decisions
☐ Punishment / Discipline   ☐ Test / Grow Our Faith
☐ God's Purpose

Reasons:

_____

_____

_____

_____

_____

Here is something to think about: Joseph was sold as a slave by his brothers, falsely accused of a crime he didn't commit, and forgotten in prison for two years after helping the Pharaoh's Cup Bearer (Genesis 45:4–7). In the end, God used these awful circumstances to help Joseph grow. Have you ever had a similar experience in which God used bad experiences for good? Talk about it with a close friend.

Helpful Resources

Genesis Apologetics

Mobile App:
Search for "Genesis Apologetics" in the iTunes or Google Play stores or visit:
http://myapp.boundarytechnology.com/promo/#Genesis%20Apologetics

Free Books and Videos:
www.debunkevolution.com
https://genesisapologetics.com/store/

YouTube Channel:
Channel Name: Genesis Apologetics

Dinosaurs:
http://genesisapologetics.com/dinosaurs

Theistic Evolution
http://genesisapologetics.com/theistic

Answers in Genesis
www.answersingenesis.org

Institute for Creation Research
www.ICR.org

Evolution Grand Experiment
www.thegrandexperiment.com

Creation Website Search Tool
www.searchcreation.org

Prayer of Salvation

You're not here by accident—God *loves* you and He *knows* who you are like no one else. His Word says:

> Lord, You have searched me and known me.
> You know my sitting down and my rising up;
> you understand my thought afar off. You
> comprehend my path and my lying down, and
> are acquainted with all my ways. For there is not
> a word on my tongue, but behold, O Lord, You
> know it altogether. You have hedged me behind
> and before, and laid Your hand upon me. Such
> knowledge is too wonderful for me; It is high, I
> cannot attain it. (Psalm 139:1–6)

God loves you with an everlasting love, and with a love that can cover all of your transgressions—all that you have ever done wrong. But you have to repent of those sins and trust the Lord Jesus Christ for forgiveness. Your past is in the past. He wants to give you a new future and new hope.

But starting this new journey requires a step—a step of faith. God has already reached out to you as far as He can. By giving His Son to die for your sins on the Cross, He's done everything He can to reach out to you. The next step is yours to take, and this step requires faith to receive His son into your heart. It also requires repentance (turning away) from sin–a surrendered heart that is willing to reject a sinful lifestyle. Many believers have a much easier time leaving sinful lifestyles after they fully trust Jesus and nobody else and nothing else. Along with forgiveness, the Holy Spirit enters your life when you receive Jesus, and He will lead you into a different lifestyle and way—a way that will lead to blessing, joy, patient endurance under trials, and eternal life with Him.

If you are ready to receive Him, then consider four key Biblical truths.

1. Acknowledge that your sin separates you from God. Most simply, sin is our failure to measure up to God's holiness and His righteous standards. We sin by things we do, choices we make, attitudes we show, and thoughts we entertain. We also sin when we fail to do right things or even think right thoughts. The Bible also says that all people are sinners: "there is none righteous, not even one." No matter how good we try to be, none of us does right things all the time. The Bible is clear, "For all have sinned and come short of the glory of God" (Romans 3:23). Admit it. Agree with God on this one.

2. Our sins demand punishment—the punishment of death and separation from God. However, because of His great love, God sent His only Son Jesus to die for our sins: "God demonstrates His own love for us in this: While we were still sinners, Christ died for us" (Romans 5:8). For you to come to God you have to get rid of your sin problem. But, in our own strength, not one of us can do this! You can't make yourself right with God by being a better person. Only God can rescue us from our sins. He is willing to do this not because of anything you can offer Him, but **just because He loves you**! "He saved us, not because of righteous things we had done, but because of His mercy" (Titus 3:5).

3. It's only God's grace that allows you to come to Him—not your efforts to "clean up your life" or work your way to Heaven. You can't earn it. It's a free gift: "For it is by grace you have been saved, through faith—and this not from yourselves, it is the gift of God—not by works, so that no one can boast" (Ephesians 2:8–9). Will you accept this gift?

4. For you to come to God, the penalty for your sin must be paid. God's gift to you is His son, Jesus, who paid the debt for you when He died on the Cross. "For the wages of sin is death, but the gift of God is eternal life in Jesus Christ our Lord" (Romans 6:23). God brought Jesus back from the dead. He provided the way for you to have a personal relationship with Him through Jesus. Trust Him. Pursue Him.

When we realize how deeply our sin grieves the heart of God and how desperately we need a Savior, we are ready to receive God's offer of salvation. To admit we are sinners means turning away from our sin and selfishness and turning to follow Jesus. The Bible word for this is "repentance"—to change our thinking to acknowledge how grievous sin is, so our thinking is in line with God's.

All that's left for you to do is to accept the gift that Jesus is holding out for you right now: "If you confess with your mouth, 'Jesus is Lord,' and believe in your heart that God raised him from the dead, you will be saved. For it is with your heart that you believe and are justified, and it is with your mouth that you confess and are saved" (Romans 10:9–10). God says that if you believe in His son, Jesus, you can live forever with Him in glory: "For God so loved the world that He gave his one and only Son, that whoever believes in him shall not perish, but have eternal life" (John 3:16).

Are you ready to accept the gift of eternal life that Jesus is offering you right now? Let's review what this commitment involves:

- I acknowledge I am a sinner in need of a Savior. I repent or turn away from my sin.

- I believe in my heart that God raised Jesus from the dead. I trust that Jesus paid the full penalty for my sins.

- I confess Jesus as my Lord and my God. I surrender control of my life to Jesus.

- I trust Jesus as my Savior forever. I accept that God has done for me what I could never do for myself when He forgives my sins.

If it is your sincere desire to receive Jesus into your heart as your personal Lord and Savior, then talk to God from your heart. Here's a suggested prayer:

> *Lord Jesus, I know that I am a sinner and I do not deserve eternal life. But, I believe You died and rose from the grave to make me a new creation and to prepare me to dwell in your presence forever. Jesus, come into my life, take control of my life, forgive my sins and save me. I am now placing my trust in You alone for my salvation and I accept your free gift of eternal life.*

If you've prayed this prayer, it's important that you take these three next steps: First, go tell another Christian! Second, get plugged into a local church. Third, begin reading your Bible every day (we suggest starting with the book of John). Welcome to God's forever family!

Endnotes

[1] Tozer, A. W. The Knowledge of the Holy. San Francisco, Calif.: Harper Collins Publishers, 1961.

[2] Fricke, Cassandra. "American Black Bear. Klamath Inventory and Monitoring Network Featured Creatures." (2021). National Park Service. *www.nps.gov/articles/000/american-black-bear.htm#:~:text=Black%20bears%20are%20omnivorous%2C%20meaning ,fruit%2C%20sedges%2C%20and%20insects*. Accessed August 5, 2022.

[3] National Wildlife Federation, "Grizzley Bear." (2022). *www.nwf.org/Educational-Resources/Wildlife-Guide/Mammals/Grizzly-Bear.* Accessed August 29, 2022

[4] Kennedy, Jennifer. "What Do Polar Bears Eat?" Posted April 17, 2019. ThoughtCo *www.thoughtco.com/what-do-polar-bears-eat-2291919.* Accessed August 5, 2022.

[5] Thomas, Brian. "Why Would God Make Monsters?" Posted November 30, 2018. Institute for Creation Research. *www.icr.org/article/why-would-God-make-monsters.* Accessed August 15, 2022.

[6] McArthur, John. "What Is Sin?" Posted January 30, 2000. Grace to You Ministries. *www.gty.org/library/sermons-library/90-233/what-is-sin.* Accessed August 5, 2022.

[7] Harold, Lindsay, and Daniel A. Biddle. The Bible & Science on Gender, Sex and Marriage, Folsom, CA: Genesis Apologetics, 2022

[8] Leggat, Iain. "What year was 9/11? When September 11 terror attacks happened-as we remember it on 20 year anniversary" Posted September 8, 2021. Nationalworld.com. *www.nationalworld.com/news/world/what-year-was-911-when-september-11-terror-attacks-happened-as-we-remember-it-on-20-year-anniversary-3348633.* Accessed August 29, 2022.

[9] Strand, Paul. "Finding God in the Shadow of 9/11: A Survivor's Story." Posted September 9, 2019. CBN News. *www1.cbn.com/cbnnews/us/2019/september/finding-god-in-the-shadow-of-9-11-a-survivors-story.* Accessed August 29, 2022.

[10] Babakhan, Jen. "9/11 Survivor Stories: Twists of Fate That Saved These People's Lives." Updated: September 8, 2021. Reader's Digest. *www.rd.com/list/twists-of-fate-saved-peoples-lives-9-11/.* Accessed August 29, 2022.

[11] Vujicic, Nick. "Meet Nick." Life Without Limbs Ministry. *www.lifewithoutlimbs.org/about/nick-biography/* Accessed August 15, 2022.

[12] Ibid.

[13] Swindoll, Charles. "Improving Your Serve: The Art of Unselfish Living." Word Books, 1981.

Made in the USA
Coppell, TX
16 September 2022

83219287R00039